Numbers

A collection of 32 mathematical puzzles

John Parker

Contents

page 3   Useful Rules

page 3   Useful Number Sequences

page 4   Level A: Puzzles 1-4

page 5   Level B: Puzzles 5-10

page 11 Level C: Puzzles 11-16

page 17 Level D: Puzzles 17-20

page 21 Level E: Puzzles 21-26

page 26 Level F: Puzzles 27-32

page 30 Solutions

page 32 How to create your own cross-number puzzles

TarquinGroup
www.tarquingroup.com

Useful Rules

Part of the enjoyment of working with numbers is to find patterns, simple rules and properties which the numbers obey. For instance most people know that the sum of the digits of any number with divides by 3 is also a multiple of 3, that multiples of 5 end in 0 or 5 and that multiples of any number may be found by repeated addition (a process made easy by using the 'repeat' or 'k' facility on most calculators). However there are many other such rules and it is interesting to find them out.

A square number never ends in 2,3,7 or 8.

Twice a triangular number always ends in 0,2 or 6.

The sum of the digits of a multiple of 9 is itself a multiple of 9.

If a cube number has an exact square root, the the root is itself a cube.

No three digit square number has a middle digit of 1 or 3.

In these puzzles no answer starts with a zero.

Useful Number Sequences

Many of the puzzle clues make use of such well-known expressions as odd, even or multiple. Other clues mention number sequences which have names. In case any of the names are unfamiliar, the list below will serve as a useful reminder. You might find it helpful to compile longer lists and to keep them to hand for the later puzzles.

Prime Numbers
2, 3, 5, 7, 11, 13, 17, 19, 23, etc.

Square Numbers
1, 4, 9, 16, 25, 36, 49, 64, 81, etc.

Cube Numbers
1, 8, 27, 64, 125, 216, 343, 512, etc.

Fourth Power Numbers
1, 16, 81, 256, 625, 1296, 2401, etc.

Triangular Numbers
1, 3, 6, 7, 10, 15, 21, 28, 36, 45, etc.

Tetrahedral Numbers
1, 4, 10, 20, 35, 56, 84, 120, etc.

Fibonacci Numbers
1, 1, 2, 3, 5, 8, 13, 21, 34, 55 etc.

Palindromic Numbers
11, 22, .., 121, 343, .., 1221, etc.

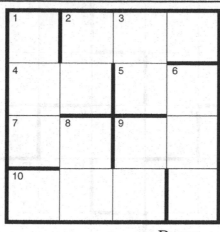

Across

2. 200 + 3 + 50
4. A multiple of 7
5. 7 x 8
7. 110 - 11
9. 8 x 3
10. 137 - 9

Down

1. 840 - 1
2. A square number
3. A multiple of 11
6. 483 + 161
8. 46 + 46
9. A triangular number

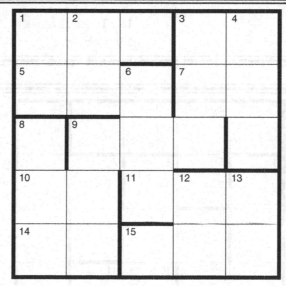

Across

1. 900 - 1
3. A triangular number
5. 190 - 19
7. A square number
9. 378 x 2
10. A square number
11. 2 + 70 + 300
14. 7 x 9
15. 1,001 - 77

Down

1. A square number
2. A prime number
3. 468 x 2
4. 334 ÷ 2
6. 170 - 17
8. *6 down + 9 down*
9. 830 - 37
12. 9 x 8
13. Number of hours in a day

3

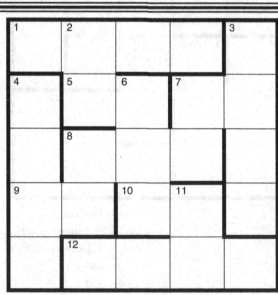

1	2		3	4
5		6		
7	8		9	
10	11		12	13
14		15		

Across
1. 13 x 9
3. 3 x 9
5. Number of weeks in a year
6. 9 x 24
8. 37 x 9
10. 76 x 9
12. 14 x 3
14. 9 x 6
15. Twice *7 down*

Down
1. *12 across - 3 across*
2. 41 x 3
3. A quarter of *11 down*
4. 85 x 9
6. 26 x 9
7. Number of days in a non-leap year
9. 7 x 7 x 7
11. Twice *12 across*
13. One score

4

1	2			3
4	5	6	7	
	8			
9		10	11	
	12			

Across
1. 10,368 ÷ 3
5. A quarter of *11 down*
7. 13 x 7
8. *3 down* ÷ 3
9. *11 down* ÷ 2
10. One-third of 87
12. *4 down* ÷ 4

Down
2. 126 ÷ 3
3. *1 across* ÷ 3
4. 16,976 ÷ 4
6. One-third of 1,446
7. 282 ÷ 3
8. 114 ÷ 3
11. *8 across* ÷ 4

5

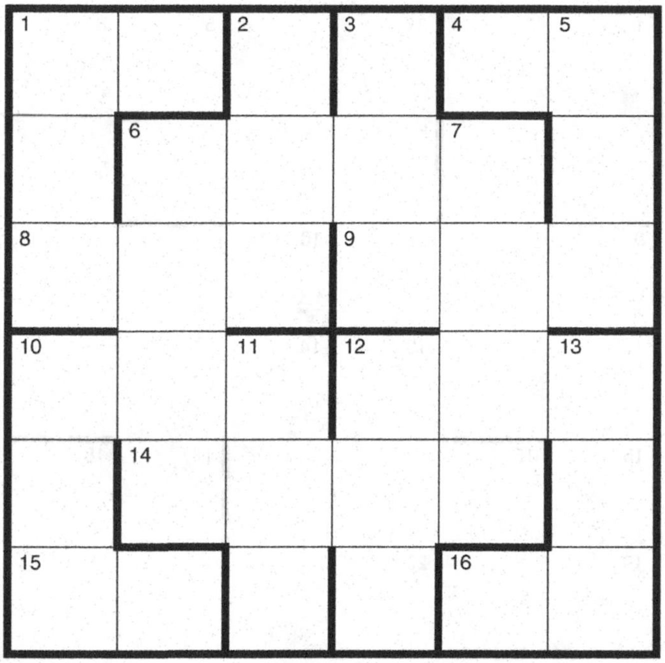
1
2
3
4
5
6
7
8
9
10
11
12
13
14
15
16

Across

1. The 10th prime number
4. A factor of *15 across*
6. 6^4
8. 6 x 22
9. 1,001 - 56
10. 675 ÷ 5
12. 11 x 19
14. Number of mm in a metre
15. The 26th even number
16. 2^5

Down

1. 10,000 - 9,799
2. 2×19^2
3. (20 + 1) x (20 - 1)
5. $13^2 + 14^2$
6. 11^3
7. 256 x 25
10. 1,000 ÷ 8
11. 113.78 + 394.22
12. Number of days in 29 weeks
13. $3^5 \times 2^2$

1	2	3	4	5	6
7		8			
9			10	11	
12		13	14		
15	16			17	18
19		20			

Across

1. 11 x 11 x 11
5. ¾ as a percentage
7. 2^5 x 3
8. Number of grams in 2 kg
9. Number of cm in 3 metres
10. 75 + 76 + 77 + 78 + 79 + 80 + 81
12. Number of days in 58 weeks
14. A multiple of 47
15. Number of pence in £16
17. A square number
19. 2^3 x 3
20. 547 x 18

Down

1. The eighth prime number
2. Number of seconds in 1 hour
3. Number of metres in 0.32 km
4. A triangular number
5. 35 ÷ ½
6. 5,313 - 246
9. 853 x 4
11. 1,221 ÷ ¼
13. 50,000 - 49,391
14. 10,896 ÷ 12
16. A square number
18. 2^4

1	2	3	4	5	6
7		8			
9				10	
11		12	13		14
15	16		17	18	
19			20		

Across

1. A multiple of 71
4. $3,992 \div 8$
7. A prime number
8. 36^2
9. $4 \times 9 \times 23$
10. The 11th prime number
11. $2^3 \times 11$
13. A square number
15. $2,973 - 1,589$
18. 16a when a = 6
19. $120\frac{1}{2} \times 8$
20. Number of cm in 5 metres

Down

1. $3,484 \div 13$
2. 12^3
3. Number of days in May
4. $106 \div \frac{1}{4}$
5. $3,213 - 3,114$
6. 31^2
10. Number of metres in 3.89 km
11. 91×9
12. Total number of days in May, June, July, August, September and October
14. Number of seconds in 16 minutes
16. A square number
17. The 9th triangular number

¹	²	³	⁴	⁵	
⁶			⁷		⁸
⁹		¹⁰	¹¹		
¹²	¹³			¹⁴	
¹⁵		¹⁶	¹⁷		¹⁸
¹⁹		²⁰			

Across

2. A multiple of *14 across*
5. *5 down - 13 down*
6. A multiple of 37
7. An even number
9. A square number
10. 459 x 7
12. 599 x 8
14. A multiple of 3
15. A factor of 3,395
17. Number of metres in 32,800 cm
19. 100 - 33
20. *5 down - 8 down*

Down

1. A multiple of 9
2. 1,872 ÷ 8
3. 477 x 7
4. Number of minutes in ¾ hour
5. A multiple of 21
8. A multiple of 17
9. A multiple of 19
11. 279 x 8
13. A multiple of 259
14. 738 ÷ 6
16. Number of hours in 4 days
18. A square number

1	2		3		4	5

Across

1. Interior angle of a regular hexagon
3. The 14th cube number
6. Number of degrees a minute hand turns through in a day
9. A multiple of 13
10. A square number
12. A triangular number
13. Number of edges on a cube
15. 214.499 correct to the nearest whole number
16. The 16th odd number
19. Number of seconds in ¾ minute
20. Number of degrees in 7 right angles
22. Number of tenths in 7.0
23. Number of hours in one-fifth of a year
25. Number of metres in 5.12 km
26. Number of days in 34 weeks

Down

1. A palindromic number
2. Number of weeks in half a year
3. Twice half a score
4. A cube number
5. A multiple of 9
7. Number of cm in the perimeter of a rectangle 13.5 x 11 cm
8. The 18th square number
11. Number of square cm in the area of a circle radius 14 cm (to the nearest whole number)
14. A fourth power
15. The 22nd triangular number
17. 12 dozen dozen
18. A quarter of 1,100
21. A factor of 333
23. Number of hundredths in one tenth
24. The 16th prime number

1	2		3	4	5
6		7	8		
9		10	11		
	12			13	
14		15	16		17
18		19			

Across

1. 37 x 66
4. 3,696 ÷ 66
6. Number of minutes in 3¼ hours
8. A multiple of 89
9. *5 down* ÷ 140
10. *9 down* ÷ 15
12. Number of hours in 3 weeks
13. Number of minutes in ½ hour
14. A square number
16. *8 across - 6 across*
18. Number of weeks in a year
19. A multiple of 9

Down

1. A triangular number
2. A multiple of 31
3. A square number
4. Number of pence in £5.31
5. Number of metres in 6.44 km
7. 10 x *18 across*
9. Number of cm in 42.15 metres
11. 3 x *10 across*
12. Number of 2p in £10.84
13. A multiple of 37
15. A square number
17. A prime number

ACROSS

2. 74 x 9
4. 1,000 ÷ 62.5
5. 19^2 x 4
7. A square number
9. Number of minutes in 2¾ hours
11. A multiple of 11
12. A prime factor of *2 across*
14. (13 x *12 across*) + 20
15. 360 ÷ 5
16. 21^3
19. Number of 5p in £2
20. A factor of *8 down*

DOWN

1. A square number
2. A cube number
3. 23 x 28
4. Number of minutes in a day
6. A triangular number
8. Number of 2p in £18.42
9. A factor of *14 across*
10. Number of grams in 6.32 kg
13. A multiple of 61
14. Number of weeks in a year
17. A prime factor of 2,211
18. A factor of *3 down*

1	2	3	4		5
	6		7		
8	9	10	11		12
13			14		
15		16		17	
18			19		

Across

1. A factor of *7 across*
3. A cube number
6. 1,000 ÷ 8
7. A multiple of *1 across*
8. A multiple of 7
10. The last year which was a square number
13. Number of 20p in £324
14. Number of cm in 0.72 metres
15. Number of hours in 2 days
16. A multiple of 11
18. Number of minutes in a day
19. A score

Down

1. A multiple of *7 across*
2. Number of days in March
3. A multiple of 101
4. Three-quarters as a percentage
5. A prime number
7. Number of days in *8 across* weeks
9. Number of hours in a week
11. Number of metres in 9 km
12. Number of grams in 6.22 kg
15. A prime number
16. A cube and a square number
17. Number of weeks in a year

Across

1. A multiple of *2 down*
3. A multiple of 11
6. The last year that was a square number
8. A factor of *1 down*
9. Number of grams in ¼ kg
11. A factor of *10 down*
13. A square number
15. Number of 20p in £181
17. 30% of 300
18. A multiple of 22
20. $19^2 + 7^3$
21. Number of articles in a gross

Down

1. A multiple of 14
2. A square number
3. A triangular number
4. Number of metres in 7.5 km
5. Number of degrees in a circle
7. 15% of 200
10. Number of cm in 56 metres
12. A multiple of 9
14. A square number
15. A triangular number
16. Number of hours in 3 weeks
19. The next number in the pattern
16, 23, 30, 37, . . .

1	2	3	4	5	6
7		8	9		
10		11	12		13
	14			15	
16		17	18		
19				20	

Across

1. A fifth power
3. A fourth power
7. A multiple of 13
9. A square number
10. A prime number
11. The square of *10 across*
14. A multiple of 37
15. A triangular number and a multiple of 13
16. A multiple of *15 across*
18. $5^4 + 5^2$
19. A cube
20. A multiple of 8

Down

1. A multiple of 101
2. A multiple of 11, a triangular number
4. The cube root of 13,824
5. A multiple of 9
6. A sixth power
8. A multiple of 11
12. πr^2 when r = 14 (to the nearest whole number)
13. A multiple of 106
14. $13^2 - 6^2$
15. $28^2 - 10\ across$
16. A triangular number
17. A prime number

A puzzle with a Christmas theme

Across

1. A prime number
3. A multiple of *1 across*
7. Year in which a King of England was crowned on Christmas Day, a multiple of *20 across*
8. Number of days in December
9. A multiple of *13 across*
11. The square of the date of Christmas Eve
13. The square of the number of pipers piping
15. A multiple of *20 across*
16. The number of wise men x the number of gold rings
17. The square of one-seventh of 19 x 21
19. The number of maids a-milking x the number of ladies dancing x the number of lords a-leaping
20. The date of Boxing Day

Down

2. 'How many miles to Babylon?'
3. Number of days in the year 1992
4. Sum of two consecutive square numbers
5. A cube number
6. A prime factor of *3 down*
7. A multiple of 9
10. *1 across* x *6 down*
12. A multiple of 29
14. Number of pipers piping x the number of drummers drumming
15. A multiple of *8 across*
16. A prime factor of *15 across*
18. The number of geese a-laying x the number of swans a-swimming

16

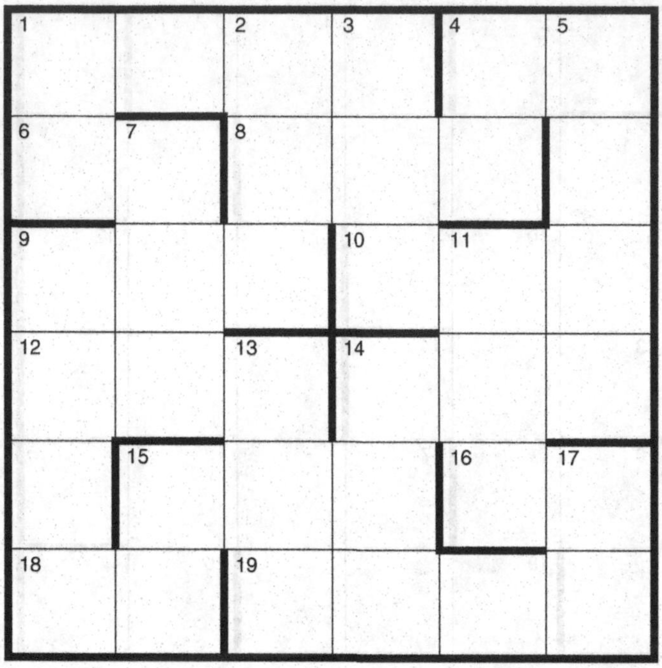
1
2
3
4
5
6
7
8
9
10
11
12
13
14
15
16
17
18
19

Across

1. A twelfth power
4. A fifth power
6. A prime number
8. A multiple of *1 down*
9. A multiple of *18 across*
10. $3x^2 - 2x$ when $x = 14$
12. A multiple of 67
14. Number of degrees on a straight line
15. $4x^2 - 3x$ when $x = 16$
16. A triangular number
18. A factor of *9 across*
19. A cube number

Down

1. A prime number
2. Twice a triangular number
3. A square number
4. Twice a prime number
5. Number of m^2 in ¼ ha
7. A cube number
9. A fourth power
11. A multiple of 11
13. A square number
14. Number of hours in a week
15. 6 x *18 across*
17. A Fibonacci number

¹	²	³	⁴	⁵	
⁶	⁷		⁸		⁹
¹⁰		¹¹	¹²		
¹³	¹⁴			¹⁵	
	¹⁶	¹⁷	¹⁸		¹⁹
²⁰		²¹			

Across

2. $x^3 + 3x^2 + 2x + 1$ when $x = 5$
5. A factor of *11 across*
6. Number of hours in two weeks
8. Number of degrees in $\frac{1}{5}$ of a circle
10. *15 across + 19 down*
11. A multiple of *5 across*
13. A square number
15. A square number
16. Number of pence in £¼
18. A multiple of 11
20. A multiple of *1 down*
21. Number of degrees in 3 right angles

Down

1. A prime number
3. $3x^3 + 2x^2 - 6x + 2$ when $x = 8$
4. A prime number
5. $2x^2 - 3x + 5$ when $x = 21$
7. Number of possible outcomes of throwing two dice
9. A factor of *12 down*
10. A multiple of *19 down*
12. A cube number
14. South-west as a bearing
15. A prime number
17. Number of playing cards in a pack
19. A factor of *10 down*

18

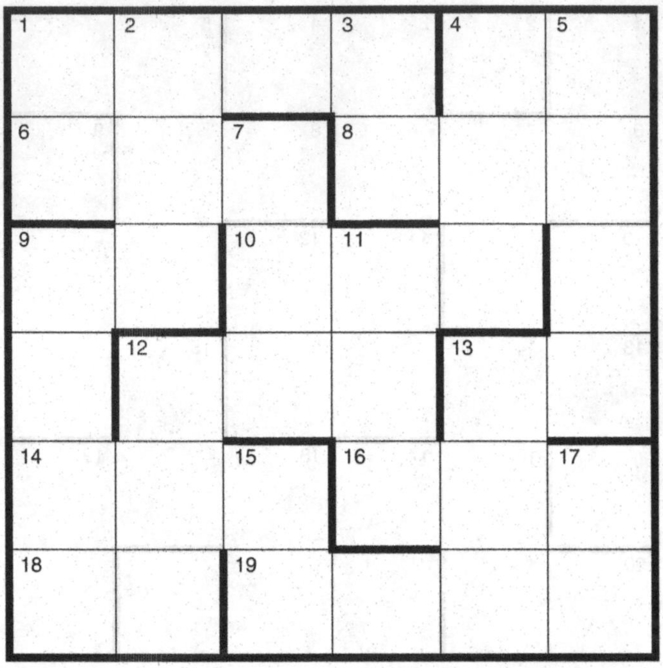

(A crossword grid with numbered cells: 1, 2, 3, 4, 5 across the top row; 6, 7, 8 in the second row; 9, 10, 11 in the third row; 12, 13 in the fourth row; 14, 15, 16, 17 in the fifth row; 18, 19 in the bottom row.)

Across

1. *4 across* × *3 down*
4. A square number
6. A square number
8. A multiple of *18 across*
9. A prime number
10. North-west as a bearing
12. Number of cm in 5.31 metres
13. Number of seconds in 1½ minutes
14. A cube number
16. A multiple of 9
18. Number of 20p in £6.40
19. Number of ml in 3.72 litres

Down

1. A multiple of 9
2. Number of metres in 0.347 km
3. Number of 5p in £3.30
4. ⅞ of 1,000
5. Number of grams in 1.25 kg
7. A multiple of 7
9. A multiple of *2 down*
11. A multiple of *9 across*
12. A multiple of *18 across*
13. A multiple of 11
15. 20% of *10 across*
17. ⅘ as a percentage

Across

2. Number of distinct ways in which 3 dice can fall
5. A cube number
8. 4 !
9. A multiple of 11
11. $2^4 \times 3 \times 5 \times 7$
13. $^2/_5$ as a percentage
14. a when a ÷ 33 = 115 ÷ 165
15. An even factor of *33 across*
17. Half as a percentage
18. A multiple of 7, 11 and 13
19. A cube number
22. A triangular number
24. Number of days in March
26. A prime number
27. Volume factor of enlargement when scale factor is 3
28. Number of seconds in 2 hr 34 min
30. A cube number
32. A factor of *25 down*
33. Number of grams in 3.5 kg
34. A multiple of *21 down*

Down

1. A multiple of 101
3. Number of sides of a regular polygon with an interior angle of 150°
4. Number of ml in 6 litres
5. A prime number
6. Number of square cm in 0.87m²
7. Number of degrees in the exterior angle of a regular decagon
10. A triangular number, a multiple of *21 down*
12. A multiple of *21 down*
13. b when 3.2 : b = 11.2 : 161
14. A multiple of 7
16. A multiple of 9
19. Number of degrees in the interior angle of a regular decagon
20. Number of degrees in *7 down* right angles
21. $x^2 + 2x - 7$, when x = 4
22. Number of 2p in £38.84
23. Number of weeks in a year
25. A fifth power
29. Area factor of enlargement when volume factor is 125
30. $3x^2 + 2x - 13.75$, when x = 3.5
31. A prime number

The grid is a crossword-number puzzle with numbered cells 1–21.

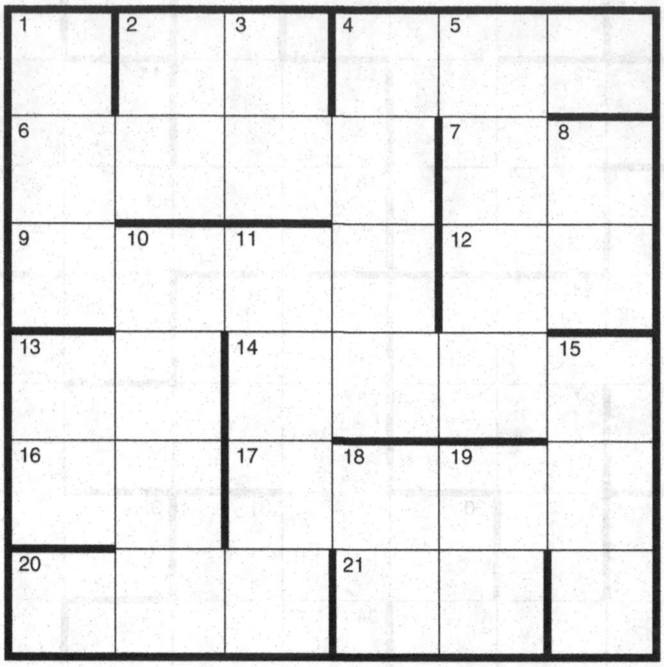

Across

2. Value of pq^2/r
   when p = 14, q = 6 and r = 12
4. Number of degrees in ¾ of a circle
6. A cube number
7. 15% of 80
9. A square number
12. The opposite bearing to 268^0
13. Twice a square number
14. A fourth power
16. The cube root of *6 across*
17. Number of hours in *2 down* days
20. Perimeter of a square
    whose area is *9 across*
21. Sin^{-1} 0.788 (to nearest whole number)

Down

1. A triangular number
2. The square root of *14 across*
3. The third number in the
   Pythagorean triple 220, 221, . . .
4. 2.314×10^3
5. Number of grams in 7.18 kg
8. A perfect number
10. Number of metres in 5⅞ km
11. Number of cm in 22.16 metres
13. A triangular number
15. A multiple of 23
18. Value of x when 3x - 2 = 2x + 13
19. The exterior angle of a
    regular pentagon

1	2	3	4	5	
6		7			8
9			10	11	
12		13	14		
15	16			17	18
19		20			

Across
2. A triangular number
5. The lowest common multiple of 3, 4 and 5
6. A prime number
7. A cube number
9. Twice a square number
10. *14 down + 17 across*
12. A multiple of 17
14. A cube number
15. An even number
17. A square number
19. 24% of 350
20. A multiple of 21

Down
1. A fourth power
2. 10 times a square number
3. A cube number
4. A multiple of 37
5. A multiple of 7
8. A multiple of *6 across*
9. One-eighth of 10^3
11. A palindromic number
13. A square number
14. A square number
16. A cube number
18. A prime number

¹	²		³	⁴	⁵
⁶		⁷			
⁸		⁹	¹⁰	¹¹	
	¹²			¹³	
¹⁴	¹⁵	¹⁶		¹⁷	¹⁸
¹⁹		²⁰			

Across

1. A multiple of the number of degrees in 1½ right angles
4. *17 across - 13 across*
6. A prime factor of *11 down*
7. A multiple of *9 across*
8. A prime factor of *1 across*
9. Interior angle of a regular 20-gon
12. Number of seconds in 3¼ minutes
13. A multiple of *6 across*
14. The cube of *15 down*
17. A prime number
19. A prime factor of *10 down*
20. Sum of the angles in a decagon

Down

1. A prime number
2. A triangular number
3. A prime factor of *2 down*
4. A multiple of *6 across*
5. A fourth power
7. A multiple of *6 across*
8. A multiple of *7 down*
10. A multiple of *19 across*
11. A Fibonacci number
15. A prime factor of *16 down*
16. A triangular number
18. A factor of the number of degrees in a circle

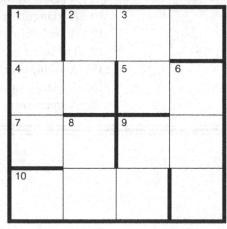

Across

1. The sum of two consecutive Fibonacci numbers
4. A cube
6. Twice a triangular number
7. The square of a factor of *14 across*
8. A Fibonacci number
10. A palindromic number
12. A prime number
14. An even number
15. The product of two consecutive prime numbers

Down

1. The square root of a triangular number
2. An odd number
3. The product of two consecutive cubes
4. Twice the square root of a Fibonacci number
5. A multiple of a composite factor of *10 across*
8. A square
9. The square of a factor of *2 down*
11. A multiple of a factor of *13 down*
13. A multiple of a factor of *4 down*

24

Across

2. Half a fourth power
4. A cube number
5. A prime number
7. Twice a square number
9. The cube root of a square number
10. A square number

Down

1. A cube number
2. A prime number
3. Twice a triangular number
6. Square root of a cube number
8. A prime number
9. A triangular number

¹	²	³	⁴	⁵	
⁶		⁷			⁸
⁹		¹⁰		¹¹	
¹²	¹³	¹⁴		¹⁵	¹⁶
¹⁷			¹⁸	¹⁹	
²⁰					

Across

2. A fourth power
6. A multiple of another *across* number
7. A multiple of *5 down*
9. Sum of the first 15 square numbers
11. A prime number
12. A composite number
14. A cube number
17. A multiple of *2 down*
19. A prime factor of *13 down*
20. A fifth power

Down

1. A multiple of *8 down*
2. *12 across* x a factor of *9 across*
3. A triangular number and a Fibonacci number
4. A multiple of a factor of *9 across*
5. A Fibonacci number which is a multiple of a factor of *15 down*
8. A prime number
10. A triangular number
12. A perfect number
13. The square of an *across* number
15. A multiple of 11
16. A triangular number
18. A square number

	1	2	3	4		5	6
7		8			9	10	
	11		12		13		
		14		15		16	
17		18		19			
20	21	22			23		
24				25			

Across

1. Half a triangular number
4. A fourth power and a cube
7. A multiple of *18 down*
8. A square number
10. Twice a triangular number
11. A prime number
12. A fifth power
14. Twice a square number
17. A cube
19. A square number
20. Twice a triangular number
22. A triangular number, ten times a triangular number
23. A prime number
24. The square of a prime number
25. A triangular number

Down

1. The square of a prime number elsewhere in the puzzle
2. A factor of *10 across*
3. A cube
5. A prime number
6. A square number
9. A factor of *14 across*
11. A sixth power
12. A cube
13. Three times a triangular number
15. A square number
16. *23 across* x the square root of *24 across*
17. A palindromic number
18. A factor of *10 across*
21. A cube
23. Three times a square number

27

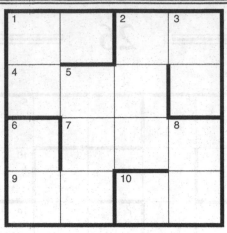

Across

1. A prime number
2. A quarter of a square number
4. A square number
7. Four times a square number
9. *7 across - 5 down*
10. A cube number

Down

1. *9 across + 8 down + 3 down*
2. A palindromic number
3. An even factor of *1 down*
5. Three times a prime number
6. *p across - q down*, also *r across - s down*
8. A prime number

28

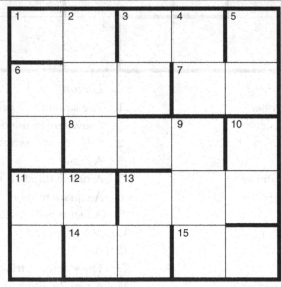

In this algebraic puzzle each letter from a to g represents a particular number, which may have 2 digits.

Across

1. bd
3. a^5
6. g(ab + d)
7. $(ab)^2$
8. a^4b^3
11. d^2
13. acf
14. e^2
15. a^3d

Down

2. f^2
3. bg
4. $a^4 + d$
5. $d^2 - b$
6. ab^2
9. $(b + f)^2$
10. ce
11. abe
12. ef
13. ad

29

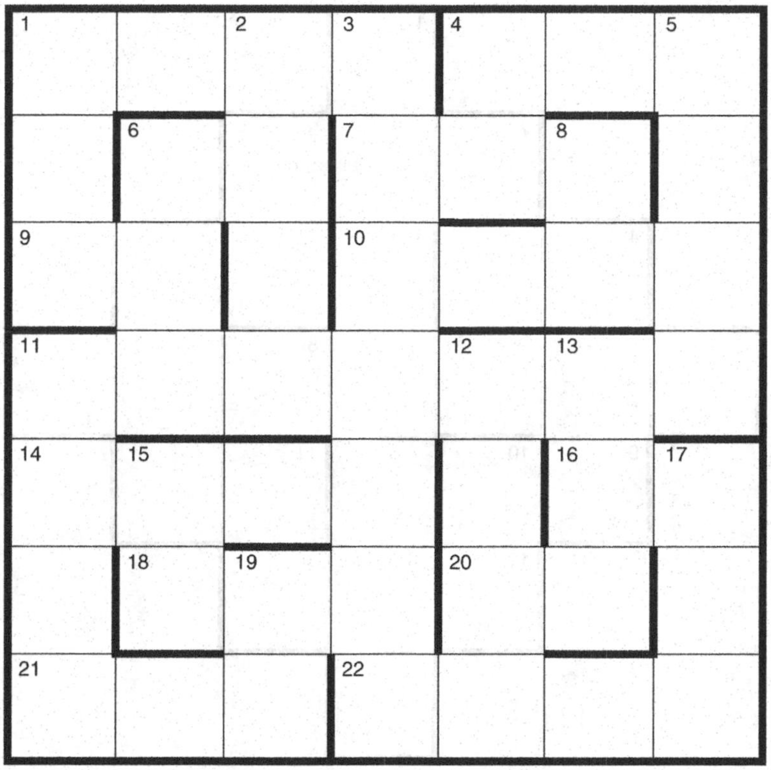

Across

1. A Fibonacci number
4. A multiple of a factor of *11 across*
6. A prime number
7. Twice a square number
9. The square root of a cube
10. A fourth power
11. A fifth power
14. *1 across + 4 across*
16. A prime number
18. A multiple of a factor of *11 across*
20. A power
21. A Fibonacci number
22. A multiple of *15 down*

Down

1. A multiple of *19 down*
2. A multiple of a factor of *11 across*
3. A sixth power
4. Twice a Fibonacci number
5. A cube number
6. Twice *13 down*
8. A factor of *18 across*
11. A multiple of a factor of *3 down*
12. A square number
13. A multiple of 8
15. A prime number
17. Twice a Fibonacci prime
19. A cube number

Across

2. Half a Fibonacci number
4. A prime number
5. A square number
7. *2 across* x *12 across* x *10 down*
9. The cube root of a square number
11. A triangular number
12. One-third of a Fibonacci number

Down

1. A multiple of the product of *8 down* and a factor of *9 across*
2. Half a square number
3. A prime number
4. A Fibonacci number
6. A multiple of *4 across*
8. A cube number
10. A multiple of 3

31

¹	²	³	⁴	⁵
⁶			⁷	
⁸	⁹			¹⁰
¹¹		¹²	¹³	
¹⁴			¹⁵	

Across

1. Twice a prime factor of *14 across*
3. A prime number
6. A triangular number
7. A prime factor of *11 down*
8. A cube
11. A square number
12. *3 across + 10 down*
14. A triangular number
15. A power

Down

1. Twice a square number
2. A prime number
3. A Fibonacci number
4. A square number
5. A factor of *10 down*
9. A square number
10. *12 across - 3 across*
11. Twice a prime number
13. A prime factor of *3 down*

32

¹	²	³	
⁴		⁵	⁶
⁷	⁸	⁹	
¹⁰			

Across

2. The cube root of a fourth power
4. The square root of a cube number
5. A prime number
7. Twice a square number
9. A square number
10. The cube root of a square number

Down

1. A cube number
2. A prime number
3. One-quarter of a square number
6. A cube number
8. A prime number
9. A triangular number

Solutions

A

1
```
8 2 5 3
3 5 5 6
9 9 2 4
1 2 8 4
```

2
```
8 9 9 9 1
1 7 1 3 6
9 7 5 6 7
4 9 3 7 2
6 3 9 2 4
```

3
```
1 1 7 2 7
5 2 2 1 6
3 3 3 3 5
6 8 4 4 2
5 4 7 3 0
```

4
```
3 4 5 6 1
4 2 4 9 1
2 3 8 4 5
4 8 2 9 2
4 1 0 6 1
```

B

5
```
2 9 7 3 1 3
0 1 2 9 6 6
1 3 2 9 4 5
1 3 5 2 0 9
2 1 0 0 0 7
5 2 8 3 3 2
```

6
```
1 3 3 1 7 5
9 6 2 0 0 0
3 0 0 5 4 6
4 0 6 9 8 7
1 6 0 0 8 1
2 4 9 8 4 6
```

7
```
2 1 3 4 9 9
6 7 1 2 9 6
8 2 8 4 3 1
8 8 1 2 8 9
1 3 8 4 9 6
9 6 4 5 0 0
```

8
```
6 2 3 4 8 4
3 3 3 5 6 2
6 4 3 2 1 3
4 7 9 2 1 8
6 7 9 3 2 8
6 7 6 2 3 1
```

9
```
1 2 0 2 7 4 4
8 6 4 0 3 9 1
8 1 9 6 2 1 4
1 2 2 1 4 3 1
2 4 5 6 3 0 7
7 0 3 1 7 5 2
5 1 2 0 2 3 8
```

10
```
2 4 4 2 5 6
1 9 5 5 3 4
4 6 2 8 1 4
2 5 0 4 3 0
1 4 4 3 3 9
5 2 9 8 3 7
```

C

11
```
8 6 6 6 1 6
1 4 4 4 4 9
1 6 5 4 4 2
6 3 7 5 0 1
7 2 9 2 6 1
4 0 3 0 7 4
```

12
```
2 3 1 7 2 8
6 1 2 5 6 9
9 1 1 9 3 6
1 6 2 0 7 2
4 8 6 0 5 2
1 4 4 0 2 0
```

13
```
1 4 7 4 7 3
1 9 3 6 5 6
2 5 0 5 0 0
2 6 4 9 0 5
9 0 8 1 4 0
7 0 4 1 4 4
```

14
```
3 2 1 2 9 6
3 3 8 4 8 4
3 1 9 6 1 1
3 1 1 1 7 8
2 3 4 6 5 0
1 3 3 1 3 2
```

15
```
3 7 3 3 3 6
1 0 6 6 3 1
7 2 6 5 7 6
1 2 1 6 5 0
1 5 3 2 4 9
3 7 2 0 2 6
```

16
```
4 0 9 6 3 2
1 3 3 2 8 5
6 4 0 5 6 0
5 3 6 1 8 0
6 9 7 6 2 8
1 6 6 8 5 9
```

Solutions

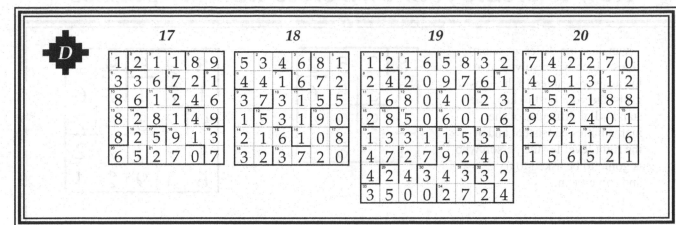

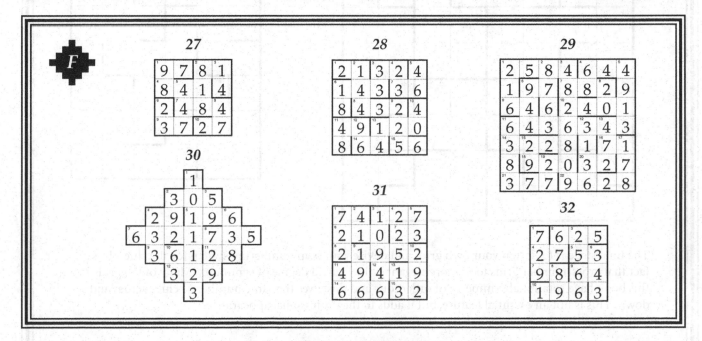

How to create your own cross-number puzzles

Try making up different sets of clues which when solved give the answers printed in these two grids. Do your best to keep the standard of difficulty of the mathematics consistent and at the right level for the person who is going to be asked to try and solve them.

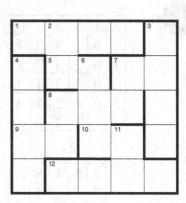

Once you have made up a suitable set of clues, blank out the numbers and then solve the puzzle yourself. It is important to make sure that there are no alternative or ambiguous answers or indeed any clues which are missing.

After that you might like to try and make up some complete puzzles. Here are four blank grids to get you started.

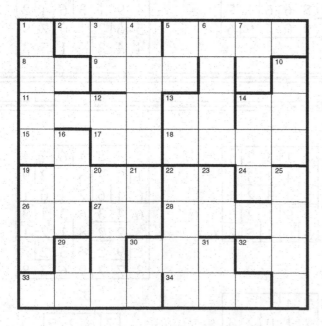

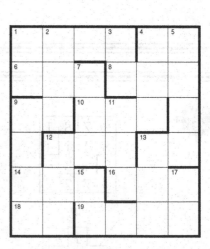

The final stage is to design your own grids and devise your own numbering system for the clues. It is a fact that cross-number grids look more elegant if they have a degree of symmetry. Many of the grids in this book have rotational symmetry of order four and this gives the same number of clues across and down. This is not an essential feature, but it adds to the professional appearance.